**TO:**_____

**FROM:**_____

Design by Anderson Thomas Design

Published by C.R. Gibson®
C.R. Gibson® is a registered trademark of Thomas Nelson, Inc.
Nashville, Tennessee 37214

Printed in Mexico.

ISBN 0-7667-6654-3
GB645R

# Our Lives Were Meant To Be Shared

photographs by
## KIM ANDERSON

poetry by
## PAULA FINN

I know you'll understand how inadequate words are

*to describe the joy and wonder I feel about us.*

When I try to define the

special meaning you've added to my life – I can't.

So I'll just say *"t h a n k   y o u"* . . .

I know you'll understand.

## YOU MAKE THE DIFFERENCE

*You make the difference*

between feeling lost, and feeling at home . . .

between listening to my fears, and following my heart . . .

between having to play a role, and feeling free to be myself . . .

between giving up on my problems and giving them another try.

*It's such a comfort to know*

that whenever the stress and demands of the outside world get us down, we can count on each other's warmth

and support to help build us back up.

We're there for each other through

the highest and lowest of times,

APPLAUDING SUCCESS,

*applauding success,*

and easing the pain of defeat;

sharing the magic of each other's dreams . . .

and working together to make them come true.

# WE ENJOY AN EASE

of relating that lets us be completely ourselves.

When we open up to reveal our innermost thoughts and secrets,

we can  *t r u s t*  each other to treat them with care.

We realize that things won't always go our way, and when we

give in a little more than we'd like it's not a defeat but an

*i n v e s t m e n t*

and we know that in choosing to share our lives . . .

sometimes we'll have to give up a little more of ourselves . . .

*to gain so much more together.*

You share my joy in the good times

and help me to see the humor in the bad times.

Your support makes everything a little easier –

And that makes a *b i g   d i f f e r e n c e .*

You listen sensitively enough to really hear me,

you look deeply enough to really see me,

*and you always make time to make me feel worthwhile.*

# YOU'RE MY BEST FRIEND –
*I can trust you...*

to show me *p a t i e n c e*

when the world is too demanding,

*a c c e p t a n c e* when others are judgmental,

loyal *s u p p o r t* when others turn away.

# I WISH YOU COULD KNOW

STRENGTH

what *s t r e n g t h* I draw from the closeness we share . . .

TRUST

the *t r u s t* I feel when I look into your eyes . . .

COMFORT

the *c o m f o r t* I feel when I hear your voice . . .

HAPPINESS

the *h a p p i n e s s* I know whenever I am with you.

I wish that I could somehow repay you

*for the gifts that have made my life complete...*

the warmth of your companionship,

the depth of your understanding,

the constancy of your support.

ASK NOTHING

*You ask nothing of me,*

yet nothing I could ever give you

could ever be too much.

# I DON'T OFTEN COMMUNICATE
*how much your support does for me...*

STABILITY

that yours is the *s t a b i l i t y* that

calms me in times of confusion,

COMFORT

the *c o m f o r t* that eases

my deepest sorrows, or the

ENCOURAGEMENT

*e n c o u r a g e m e n t* that

so often makes the difference

between giving up and giving my all.

# I DON'T OFTEN EXPRESS

*how great a difference you always make –*

by offering me open arms when I need to be held,

a listening ear when I need to be heard,

yourself – when I need to feel loved.

So what better way to thank you simply for being

the most important person in my life –

for you've done more for me

than anyone else has . . .

*and you mean more to me than anyone else will.*

When I am stubborn you see behind the charades I sometimes play,

*and gently push me toward the person I'd rather be . . .*

When I am frightened,
your comfort tells me
what I need to hear most:

I'm not alone.

When I am hurting,
I need to be reminded of the
pain my struggles create in you
for I am not used to having
someone care so much about me
that my suffering becomes theirs.

Your support means a lot...

Your love means everything.

It's comforting to know

*we can count on each other...*

to understand our most complex ideas,

and to share our deepest feelings . . .

that we can talk openly and trust

that our words won't be judged.

COMMUNICATION

Our *c o m m u n i c a t i o n* is easy,

nourishing and complete.

# MY WISHES FOR US . . .

That we'll continue to share
new interests and adventures,
and allow each other freedom
to develop as individuals as well . . .

That our faith won't be shaken by
occasional feelings of hurt or anger –
that we'll continue to acknowledge
our differences openly, and to see
them as opportunities to learn
and to grow closer . . .

That we'll find in each disagreement the patience to listen,

the courage to trust, and the strength to forgive.

We'll never forget

the qualities that first attracted us

to each other and how much we still

APPRECIATE

*appreciate them . . .*

We'll always inspire

the best in each other, applauding successes,

NURTURING

*nurturing strengths –*

believing in each other's dreams

and working as one to make them

TRUE

*come true.*

We don't know what changes lie ahead,

or where our *s h a r e d   p a t h* will lead . . .

But what I do know is that I'm here for you today –

to listen or talk, to applaud or console . . .

to want, need,

*...and to love you with all my heart.*